Don't Cry on Cashmere

Brianna Malotke

Don't Cry on Cashmere

Copyright © 2022 Brianna Malotke & The Ravens Quoth Press
First published in Australia in November 2022 by The Ravens Quoth Press

All characters and events in this publication, other than those clearly in the public domain, are fictitious and any resemblance to real persons, living or dead, is purely coincidental.

All rights reserved. No part of this production may be reproduced, stored in a retrieval system, or transmitted, in any form or by any means, electronic, mechanical, photocopying, recording or otherwise, without the prior permission of the publisher and copyright owner.
ISBN: 978-0-6454697-6-9
ISBN: 978-0-6454697-7-6

Cover design by Dawn Burdett
Formatting by Kara Hawkers
Editing by Kara Hawkers and E. Mery Blake

This collection of poems has been a work in progress for a long time. It's dedicated to everyone that I've lost in my life. From family members passing away to all the best friends who have drifted apart over the years, this is for you.

When the world seems empty and you're feeling alone, everything seems gloomy. You are not alone.

This is for everyone who doesn't think that they'll make it to the end. Someone loves you.

Brianna Malotke
November 2022

LOVE 15

    A Moment 17

    Give In 18

    Uncertain Happiness 19

    Days Past 20

    Time Passing 21

    Discovery 22

    What a Reverie 24

    Our Choices 25

    Two People 26

    Love Letters 28

    Kept Promises 29

    Found 30

    My Time 33

    Searching for Serenity 34

    Loved Completely 35

    Close to My Heart 36

    My Changing Roots 37

LOSS..39

- My Grief is Drowning 41
- Fake Smile 43
- For Two 44
- Ever Changing..46
- Drowning in My Dreams 48
- Until I Sleep 50
- Grieving 52
- Permanent Memory 54
- Unable to Leave 56
- Grief in the Moonlight 58
- Gone With the Tide..................................60
- Drifting, Unknown 62
- A Lonely Pot of Tea 64
- Waiting to Heal..66
- Don't Cry on Cashmere............................68

HOPE 71

Sunsets 73
With An Aching Heart 74
Dreaming 76
With Hope 78
Another Chance 79
Once More 80
Lost in Thoughts 82
Sitting Still 83
Just like the Trees 84
Autumn Exchanges 86
Comfort 88
At Peace 89
Past Love Notes 90
Declaration of Love 92
Alone in the Moonlight 94
On All the Petals 96
Our Fixed Future 98
Seasons Changing 100
Tears from the Night Before 102
Ready 104
Space for One 105

BRIANNA MALOTKE 109

THE RAVENS QUOTH PRESS 111

"The most beautiful things in the world cannot be seen or touched, they are felt with the heart."

– Antoine de Saint-Exupery, *The Little Prince*

Brianna Malotke

Don't Cry on Cashmere

LOVE

Brianna Malotke

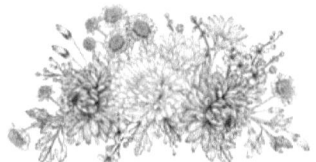

A Moment

Sitting in the cafe, listening to
The crowd around me, I'm
Enjoying my coffee and then
Time seemingly stands still
Our eyes meet, and my heart
Races—louder and louder in
my chest—I can't look away
Your emerald eyes piercing,
My mind racing, as you walk
Towards me—closer and
closer you come—I don't
Know what to say My mind
Fumbles, but when you smile
At me—you're mere feet
away from my table now—
My insides melt, my voice
Clear now, I ask you to sit
We share a smile, a moment,
It's electrifying, what a chance
We have for love to blossom.

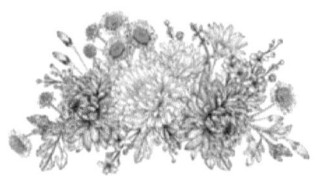

Give In

I need to feel your lips against my skin,
to feel the passion between us bloom.
I desire all of you, not just a taste,
I want nothing more than everything
With you, to give in to the passion that
Entangles my heart around yours
With every passing moment spent
In your presence my heart aches
For more—and more—time together.
When you smile, I feel as if I'm floating
Above the clouds, I'm so high I never
Want to come down, and as you press
Your lips to mine, everything else melts
Away, it's just me and you in this moment.
I want to be the reason for your joy, and
I ask you, to give in to these feelings,
For I can't imagine any other love
Than the one blossoming between us.

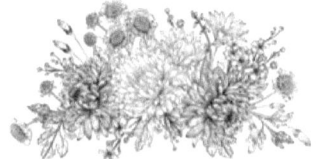

Uncertain Happiness

Ticking ticking ticking, louder now,
The clock on the wall is screaming
At me now, the seconds rush by as
You stare, waiting for my reply,
My heart beats loudly now, out of sync
With the clock on the wall, it's all
Too loud, the ticking continues, my
Mind is racing, unsure of what to do,
Unsure of what to say, I wish there was
An atlas laying out all my emotions,
Earmarking my favorite memories
Of us and highlighting the best route
For our happiness, but I don't know what
To say to you, your eyes are eager for
A "yes". My heart is pounding inside my
Chest—*tick tick tick*—my mind, my
Heart, has made its decision, but I'm
Not sure if you're ready for the answer.

Brianna Malotke

Days Past

Remembering days past
His Grecian statuesque form
His callipygian figure
Skin smooth and soft
To the touch
These memories
Of sweet moments
Intimate times past
Are hard to forget
And bittersweet to remember

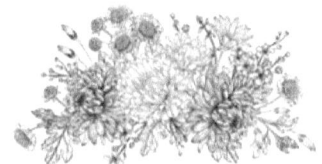

Time Passing

Dancing by twilight
Watching the fireflies flicker.

Dancing by candlelight
Watching the shadows shift.

Dancing by memory
Watching the hourglass sift.

Dancing by your side
Watching your smile spread.

Brianna Malotke

Discovery

First wonder goes deepest

My stomach in knots
I was terrified
the horror must be real
Why make dirty what is beautiful?

He was a man
—open, patient—
he would offer comfort and guidance
in case anyone should want to talk

With shine and power
and might
This Son is a god who died

I couldn't get Him out of my head
I asked questions
The answer was always the same
Love

I thought I would explode with joy.

Brianna Malotke

What a Reverie

Her favorite flowers were tulips
Preferably yellow, like lemons and citrine,
And her eyes sparkled when she spoke
About her passions, especially baking.
And my bitter heart skipped a beat when
She shared with me her favorite bench
In the park we both frequented, joking
About how we both had the same lipstick
Shade on. I could listen to her laugh all day,
This lovely ethereal daydream of a woman

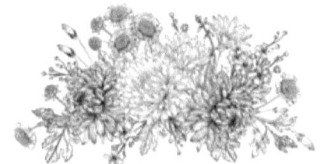

Our Choices

The world is an ugly place
> *my Darling go to bed and*

it's full of disgust
> *ponder the stars*

for the world is polluted
> *your mind is pure*

and people distrust others while you
> *believe in hope and think of new things*

make hard decisions
> *make wishes and dream*

those around you have smirks
and greed on their faces
> *and smile for me*

you must make choices
but then
> *go to bed and ponder the stars*

we all must make choices

Brianna Malotke

Two People

my feet are bound
my eyes unclean
my voice a whisper
my words mean

my tongue twisted
my hands tied
my mind in chaos
my words lies.

you unravel the ribbon
around my eyes
unknot the phrases,
the coiled up lies.

my heart racing
pounding in my chest
my body breaking
my eyes clearing

your eyes sparkling
your touch calming
my nerves easing
my mind peaceful.

no longer complicated
no longer confusing
no lies, no hate
no longer just me.

Brianna Malotke

Love Letters

You squeezed my hand three times.
Without words, telling me—*I love you.*

We didn't know when we'd see each
other again, my words caught in my throat.
With one last embrace, you left.

Over the years we exchanged letters,
allowing us to fill the pages with expressions
of affection, secrets, musings of our days,
and even our sorrows.

Through paper we shared everything.
Oceans were in between us, one
day we'll be face to face again

And when it happens, we'll have the courage
to give those sacred words a voice—*I love you.*

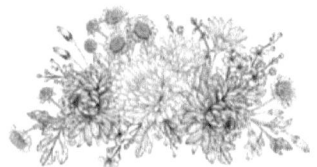

Kept Promises

With the shooting star above us,
We each made a wish and a promise.
No matter where our travels took us,
We would remain together.

Every single night spent without you
In my bed makes my heart feel hollow.
The emptiness such a stark contrast
To the warmth and joy you bring to my life.
Yet we continue on, upholding that promise
We made all those years ago.

One day we'll lay down roots together,
We'll build a home and grow old
Together, we're hopeless romantics
Who made a promise years ago.

Brianna Malotke

Found

My body slowly drifting away
My eyes go heavy and start
to close shutting the world out
One by one my limbs are turning
 numb and fading away

It's as if someone
is turning the temperature down
and my heart is the knob
slowly, quietly the ice spreads
encasing my heart
traveling sluggishly
through my veins
Like a deadly virus taking its time
The ice numbs the pain
The ice cools my burning pain
The ice makes me peaceful

Almost

My mind begins to wander
My mind begins to thaw
I can't control it
Spreading like a wildfire
Hungry for destination
Thawing my numbness
Attacking the virus
Taking hold on the knob
Coursing through my veins
This passion
This feeling
This love is quickly moving
Picking up its pace
It's already won

Brianna Malotke

My eyes flit open
My eyes dart around
My eyes meet yours
My mind found the cause
Of the fiery army overtaking me

Your lips met mine

As simple as that
My pain is gone
My numbness has disappeared
My love has only grown
Hopefully you can contain it

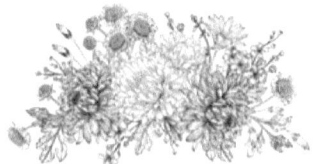

My Time

The tranquility of the evening,
With the fireflies flickering and
The crickets and the birds chirping
Away, this quintessential Fall
Night is a picturesque moment.

Just the two of us, watching the
Sun drift over the horizon, with
Cotton candy-colored clouds
And the slight wind rustling
Small leaves around our feet,
I've never felt more content
With life than now, with you.

Sometimes I'm worried that life
Will fly right by us, but then
Your smile melts any fears away,
And my anxious heart relaxes,
And I relish this time with you.

Brianna Malotke

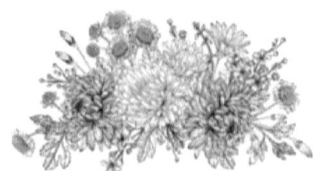

Searching for Serenity

That little bit of serenity, always
Seemingly just out of reach, is
Something we find ourselves
Always striving for, and while
Looking for that bit of happiness
I've found you, amongst all the
Thorns and dead flowers, I've
Found a sense of harmony and
Ease when I'm spending time
With you, and for this I will
Always cherish every single
Little passing moment together.

You are my serenity among chaos.

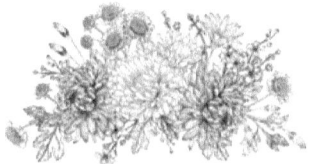

Loved Completely

Overly flowery, the scents,
Unable to separate them out,
Were much too overwhelming,
But as she held the bundle of
Unknown flowers and greenery
In her hands, she looked deep
Into her partner's eyes, and felt
Loved completely, for her entire
Being—mind, body, and her
soul—and with such powerful
Feelings, how could she not smile
Back, silently thanking the old
Fates for putting them together.

Brianna Malotke

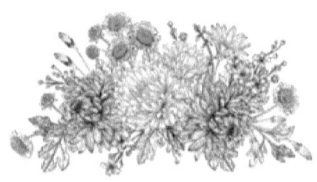

Close to My Heart

Your presence in my life,
Hopefully not fleeting, is
Something so welcome.

It brings a smile to my face,
Like a homemade apple pie
Or hug from a friend you
Haven't seen in a long time.

I'll keep the memories we
Made close to my heart
For as long it keeps beating.

A first love is such a magical
Experience, and I'm very
Thankful you were mine,
A treasure for the ages.

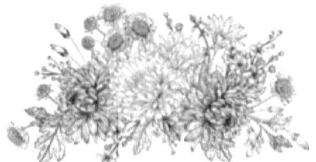

My Changing Roots

I've never been afraid of loneliness
It's something I had assumed would
Be a part of my life, for days on end,
And so, I grew accustomed to being
A party of one, for all of eternity.
But then I met you, and your smile
Your laughter, everything about
Your kind soul, found its way through
My thorny self. Your roots grew
Around mine, gently changing their
Ways, until ours were wound
Together—so perfectly—and we
Were one in a way I've never known
Before, but I have begun to welcome
With arms wide open. For how could
I imagine a world without you, my
Soulmate, my eternal happiness.

Brianna Malotke

Don't Cry on Cashmere

LOSS

Brianna Malotke

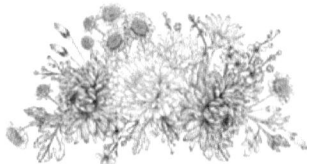

My Grief is Drowning

Those first days after I lost you,
I felt like my soul was on fire.
That my nerves had been torched
And the fire only grew within me
Stronger and stronger. My voice
Hoarse, until the screaming stopped.
And my lungs, were blackened now
From the smoke of burnt memories.

And then I was numb, floating
In the cool waters of my misery.
The tears no longer came, my eyes
Dry, and the salty taste disappeared.
And now everything was garbled,
The voices around me mumbling.
And I'm drowning in my sadness,
Letting the darkness take me whole.

Brianna Malotke

Deeper and deeper in the water
I submerge myself, the ice flowing
Through my veins, filling my being,
And I'm drowning, now just alone,
My grief from losing you too much.
And I'm drowning, I hold my breath,
Letting those memories fade away
With my last breath, as I drown.

Fake Smile

A smile on her face

The words on repeat

The whispers echo in her bones

The doctors' words on repeat

Her screams do echo in her soul

A smile on her face

Brianna Malotke

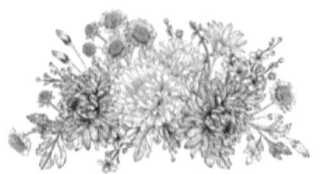

For Two

Side by side
With nothing to say
Staring at stars
Shining brighter than usual.

Both aware of
Time that's been wasted
Love that's been misplaced
But feelings hung around.

Side by side
Fingers interlaced
Embracing the cold air
And the calm of the night.

For some,
It's a very simple secret:
Loneliness can still be felt
Even when among others.

Side by side
With nothing to say
They let the night air
Embrace them until day.

Brianna Malotke

Ever Changing

The shape of a hopeful sleeper
casts a soft shadow.

I wished a wish
on all five petals.

A falling leaf catches moonlight,
the lovers still.

Withered roses fill the light
love, you can see.

Sky darkens, one odor changes
wild roses throughout the air.

A hot night, out of season—
first frost covers the ground.

September rain, fallen leaves
drifting, and withered roses.

Rampaging thunderstorms shake the window
pane, a lonely witness.

Suicide point, the bridge's cables vanish
she wakes in a sweat.

The shape of a brokenhearted
sleeper casts a stark shadow.

Brianna Malotke

Drowning in My Dreams

Lately I'm drowning in my dreams,
The water cold against my bare skin,
My breathing shallow until the strong
Waves overtake me. My struggling
Is for naught, the murky ocean waters
Swallow me whole. My body ice now,
My lungs frozen from the salt water
I've consumed in my struggles. The
Darkness has come to collect me,
My body—and my soul—but still
I fight. I thrash in the inky black
Waters, the unknown haunting me,

Pulling me deeper—and deeper –
Beneath the surface. Then, when I think
My heart has stilled, my breathing
Slow and I'm about to lose myself,
I wake up—alone—in my bed.

Lately I'm drowning in my dreams,
And one day I fear that I won't wake.

Brianna Malotke

Until I Sleep

Speak softly

My nightmares are screaming.

They claw

They scratch

Waiting for an opening.

In the silence

Of the night they're free.

Free to soak

Into my soul

Until that peaceful sleep.

My nightmares,

While my soul is weak,

They do creep

Into my bones.

Until my eyes are heavy
And my mind weary
My nightmares
They do scream.

Until my heart beats slowly
And my body is still
My nightmares
They do scream.

Until in slumber
With peaceful dreams
And sleep as deep as oceans
My nightmares

They do scream.

Brianna Malotke

Grieving

She sat all in black

Picking at the pills on her wool skirt

Nose red

Cheeks flushed

Head pounding from

The constant tears

Wind rustled the leaves around her worn heels

The scratches seemed so unimportant now

Her outlook on what was important

Had been changing

She knew the priest was talking

And that those around her were standing

By her, guarding, waiting

Don't Cry on Cashmere

If she broke, they'd be there
She was waiting to be alone
For those who had been hovering
The last few days to leave

She wanted to be alone
With her thoughts
And her grief

Brianna Malotke

Permanent Memory

Still ensorcelled
After all these years

Her memories of him
Would be there
Ever present in her mind.

His booming laugh
His soft smile
The way his eyes
Would sparkle
When he spoke
Passionately.

She stood on her balcony
And she sighed
As she took a drag
Of her third cigarette

She let the cool damp air
Surround her
As her memories
Ever present
In her mind
Made a permanent home.

After all these years
Without him there
She was still ensorcelled.

Brianna Malotke

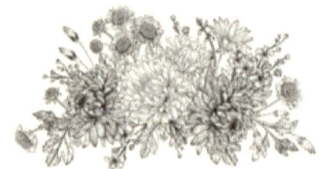

Unable to Leave

My tear, and rain, soaked dress
Had seen better days, but so too
Had my soul. And now as I stand
Alone amongst the trees and other
Recently filled graves, my heart
Aches and as my mascara streaks.
And the wind howls, I stand there,

Firm like the angel statues watching
Over the dead. My sadness seeping
Into every fiber of my being, and
I just stand there, because if I leave
I feel as though I may never return
To visit, the pain will be too great,
The memories too overwhelming.

For now, I stand here, the autumn
Air cold against my damp face,
My grief too heavy for me to bear.

For now, I stand here. Eventually
I'll leave you. But for now, I'm here.

Brianna Malotke

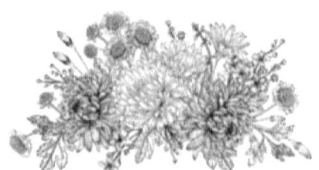

Grief in the Moonlight

Everything is heavy, this weight
That I carry with me, the memories
And feelings, everything unbearable.

My body feels as though I'm moving
Through wet sand, time slipping by
Me as I try to carry on, now alone.

The silence stretches, the house
Dark and lonely, with the shadows
Cast on the walls my only company.

Grief always seemed funny to me,
Unattainable and unimaginable, but
Now it's become another part of me.

I used to love the sunlight, feeling
The warmth against my bare skin,
But now I only crave the darkness.

Don't Cry on Cashmere

As my tears fall, my body no longer
Feels, my heart is numb to any pain
Or joy, and I succumb to my grief.

Days and months and years may
Pass, but you'll always be a part
Of me, of my heart and soul.

I don't expect to heal overnight,
But as I let the moonlight stream
In my room, I close my eyes and
Finally feel a little more at peace.

Brianna Malotke

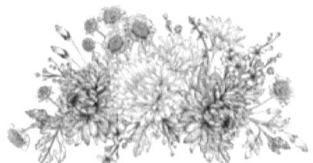

Gone With the Tide

Lost amongst the stars, my dreams
Are long gone, those little daydreams
Of you and me, dancing together
And growing old, everything is gone.
Turned to dust and scattered among
The ocean waves below, as they crash
Into the cliffs, your ashes and my dreams
Are carried out to sea, never to return
Again, and as the stars twinkle above,
My love—lost forever—is dimmed.

Brianna Malotke

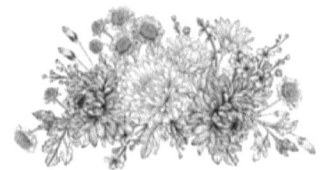

Drifting, Unknown

Falling, drifting in the wind
in the darkness, in the silence.

Her mind wondered; eyes wandered.

Decisions had to be made,
The right one unknown.
She took a deep breath and
Truly looked around her here.

The cards on the table all out of
sort, some faded from the sunlight
coffee stains on the table, the flowers
wilting, fallen petals all around.

The fluorescent lights too bright,
the bed looked uncomfortable.

Memories came flooding back to her.

She couldn't decide, just one
Choice needed but she was falling
in an ocean of tears, her weariness
too heavy to fight, she couldn't.

she couldn't picture the outcome,
their future gone, but every detail
of their time together forever
engrained in her memory.

He wouldn't want her to
Give up, to quit on them.

But he wasn't here, not really.

The doctors arrived, the room
Too small, the lights too bright,
Her voice wavered, though
Her mind made up now.

As the monitors dimmed
and the beeping ceased, she
was falling, drifting now,
and he was truly gone.

Brianna Malotke

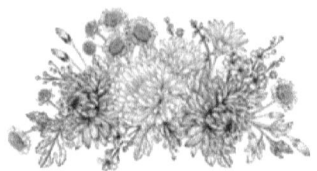

A Lonely Pot of Tea

Sun streaming in through the
Slight crack in the curtains of my
Bedroom, the rays warm on my face.

Out of bed I go, ready to start
the kettle and enjoy some currant
tea, the soothing floral notes
pleasantly starting off my day.

Everything seems nonstop, it's
Been difficult without you, and
My mind wanders, my days long,
My heart aches, tugging me down.

I try to unwind, to have a moment
Alone, with my thoughts, though
They're all full of you—your
Smiling face—and my muscles

loosen as the lively golden cup of
fresh jasmine and French lavender
fills my body, relaxing my soul,
I start to think I can carry on.

Thinking about each and every
single little detail is tiring, and
I can no longer turn to you in
Times like these. Loneliness

Envelops me, the darkness seems
To pull me in, it's cold and
Difficult to leave, but I carry on.
And turn to my kettle, with a cup

Of tea, the scents overwhelming
My senses, scooping my fragile
Soul out of the solitary confines
I had resigned myself to being.

Sitting at the table, my thoughts
And my tea, my only company,
But as I sip, I feel myself healing.

Brianna Malotke

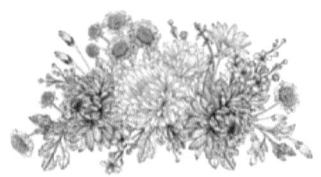

Waiting to Heal

Your letters sit, unopened
In a box beneath my bed.
Perhaps one day I'll find the
Strength that I've never felt.
Maybe one day your loss
Won't hurt me as much,
And I'll be ready to open
Myself to fresh wounds,
Letting the current ones
Become scars—ugly and
Tough—until I feel ready.
And then, maybe, I'll open
Your letters and read your
Words, but for now, as I
Sit alone in the dark, simply
Waiting for time to pass

And for my memories to
Dim—just a little bit—for
The pain to numb, letting
My soul ease into place.
For my heart was shattered
When you died, and the
Pieces unable to be put back
Properly. My loss of you
Heavy on my mind, for now.

Brianna Malotke

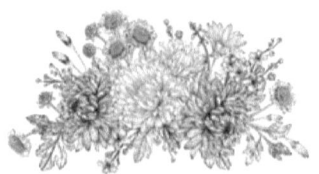

Don't Cry on Cashmere

Walking to school, the winter weather
Calming as she trekked along in snow
Through the quiet town, happily alone.

Dressed for comfort, for warmth, she
Carried on about her day, uninterested
In those around her, deep in thought.

Stomach full of knots, head full of bees,
Unable to focus or reply, she sat there,
Trying to accept the news, the grief.

As her eyes blurred, hot from tears
That started to trickle down, her main
Concern, her dry clean only cashmere.

Don't Cry on Cashmere

She would be strong, a stone pillar against
The wind and the storms, her grandmother's
Advice, her whispered words, floating by.

Standing there amongst others, the fresh
Snow crunching under each step, the
Mourners ink spills in the snow covered

Graveyard, her cashmere sweater warm,
Though soaked with tears, unable to follow
Advice, even just one last time, she smiled.

Brianna Malotke

Don't Cry on Cashmere

HOPE

Brianna Malotke

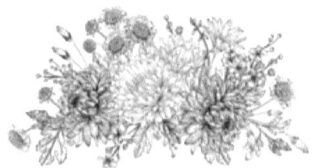

Sunsets

Sunsets always had a way
Of making her feel small
In a world of chaos

Surrounding her every move
She would watch the sun
Slowly drift down for the evening

Accepting that the moon
Would soon rise for her turn

She liked the warmth that the sun brought

But the moonlight was something else

Entirely, it brought a sense
Of ease

Brianna Malotke

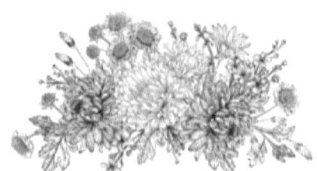

With An Aching Heart

Looking out the window, longing
For your return, the silence stretches
As I remain still, yearning for more
Time spent with you, for happiness.

All the moments we shared, etched
Into my soul, forever a part of me
And I'll carry them wherever I go,
Always wishing we'll create more.

Days pass, the sun less enjoyable
Now and my evenings spent in
Total darkness, the only sounds
Are the empty house as the wind
Howls outside, my heart aching.

I'm drifting through time, slowly
Healing as the memories of us
Fade around the edges, my heart
Repairing the damage you've done,
The future finally looking bright.

Brianna Malotke

Dreaming

Forever dreaming.

Dreaming of sun and beautiful places.
Dreaming of travels and friends.

Dreaming in French
of adventures not yet taken
of experiences waiting to happen.

Dreaming.
Dreaming.
Dreaming.

Hoping that someday,
at some point,
they'll come true.

Dreaming and hoping

that I'll soon be practicing my French
with native speakers and sipping coffee
while enjoying a fresh baked pastry
from a colorful patisserie
with friends.

Dreaming so much
that I'll just have to find a way
to make them all true.

Forever dreaming.

Brianna Malotke

With Hope

Strong-willed, we parted our separate ways,
But still, there's a part of me that wishes we
Remained together. You're always on my
Mind though, your smile, your laugh, your
touch—and you're all I can think about. Some
Days it's easier to carry on, some days it's
As if I'm merely going through the motions.
But you're always at the back of my mind,
Creeping through my memories, and a part
Of me seems to feel like you'll always be
There, a sliver imbedded in my soul. As I try
To move on from us, looking for another
Potential soulmate in life, I'm hopeful now.

Another Chance

Your laugh was melodious;
your voice like honey dripping
on my soul. I hung on every word,
every touch. My heart shattered
when you decided we should split.

Whenever I saw someone riding past
with a bundle of yellow tulips
in their bike basket, my heart ached.
I never found anyone to love quite like you.

Years later, in this crowded cafe,
I find myself staring at you
over my coffee. My heart is pounding.
You come sit next to me.
With a smile you say what
I've been dreaming about –
you're ready to give us a second chance.

Brianna Malotke

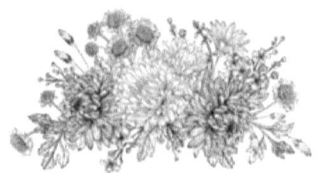

Once More

Electrifying, the air has that
Certain energy to it, I know
Now that I can do this, I'm
Already stronger now than
When I had decided to leave.

Here we go, once more, I
Want to try to work through
All the issues that you tried
To hide and shove away, but
Nothing can keep me down.

Here we go, the past has
Only helped me grow, and
Now I stand tall, ready to face
You head on, battling all my
Anxiety and buried grief.

You may not understand how
But through all the tears and
All of the heartache, I'm
Stronger now, and looking to
The future, one without you
Present in it, I say bring it on.

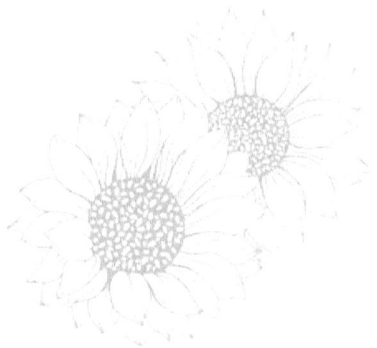

Brianna Malotke

Lost in Thoughts

Frozen—her—hands
around the once full
cup—to the bone.

She could see the snow
—she could see her breath—
outside the kitchen window.

Without noticing the day
Had—faded with horrible memories
of the night before—slipped away.

Reminding herself that
—everything—everything
was going to be okay.

Her home—was miles
Away—and her soul,
her body, were resilient.

Sitting Still

The grass was still damp
From the morning dew
But still she lies
Soaking in the sun's warmth

In the field
Surrounded by flowers
And the buzzing of small bugs
She lies still, waiting

Eyes closed
Mind wandering
She thought that maybe
Everything would be just fine.

Brianna Malotke

Just like the Trees

Pieces broken and scattered
Like the fallen, decaying leaves,
Worried she'll never be whole.

Her heart full of longing,
Yearning for those never there.

She waited night after night
Until she was finally able
To put the pieces back together.

With time and acceptance
She could be whole again.

There is darkness in life, and
Wanting a bright future, she
Would daydream all the time.

Just like the trees shaking off
Their leaves for the coming winter,
She too would discard the past.

With a scarred, yet full heart
She was ready to love again.

Brianna Malotke

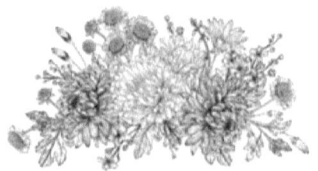

Autumn Exchanges

Breathing in the crisp autumn air
Goosebumps blossomed along
Her exposed arms, just one more
Chance to soak in a sunny day
Before the night would creep in
Earlier—and earlier—each day.

The leaves were changing colors,
Going from greens to golds,
To burnt oranges and rusty reds,
All the different shades swirling
Around her as she strolled down
The stone sidewalk path.

Passing the old Victorian homes,
The painted ladies dotting
The lane, it seemed as though
Fall was making its home here,
Nestling in every open space
It had the chance to settle.

Soon pumpkins and gourds
Would be on every front porch,
With candy apples and homemade
Pies shared among the neighbors,
She smiled to herself, happy
With the changes that would come.

Brianna Malotke

Comfort

She was lying still
with the moonlight streaming
In, filling the small room.

Stacks of books
Lined the four walls
Like a warm embrace.

Her favorites all within reach,
And a queen bed
full of pillows
And soft blankets.

She lay by herself,
In the middle of it all.

The only thing that
Could make the moment
Any better
Would be a cup of tea.

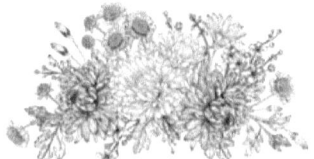

At Peace

As she sits, her mind nestled
Among the clouds, the slight
Wind picking up her hair and
The leaves and making the
Flowers dance in the sunlight.

She feels at peace here,
In this moment.

Memories would remain
Forever etched into her,
Something she would carry
Forever as she traveled, while
Her lover would remain here.

Her heart continued to beat,
And it would love again.

As long as the sun shined,
And the flowers bloomed,
She had faith in the future.

Brianna Malotke

Past Love Notes

Scrawled notes, the tiny forgotten
Memories mixed in with water
damaged photos and trinkets
from their all-consuming,
passionate romance.

Buried in a box in the closet, far
Away from her mind where he
Would remain forever, for if
She reminisced it would be
Just pain and heartache.

She had moved on, or so she
Claimed to others, but now
She didn't really think
Anyone could ever
Be forgotten.

One stormy evening, she pulled
The box out, and gently read,
And reread everything in it,
Her heart full, not broken,
She felt loved again.

Could you ever really move on
From a loved one, they will
Forever be a part of your
Story—your past and
Your future—rosy.

Brianna Malotke

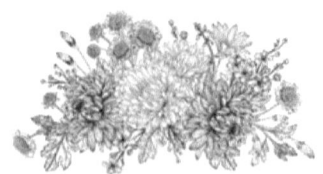

Declaration of Love

The words clung to her, every
Syllable a loud drum within
Her mind, how could someone
Love so much, and not reply.

The silence, heavier than any
Weight she ever carried,
Stretched out, lingering
Between the two of them.

Waiting, waiting, waiting.

As time slipped between them,
Certainty grew to unease, and
As those minuscule minutes
Passed by, so to had the love.

Waiting, waiting, waiting.

Separate souls, wandering
For another to connect with
And to bond together, but
Waiting isn't too bad, when
Love is at the end of it.

Brianna Malotke

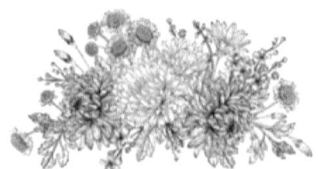

Alone in the Moonlight

Sunrises never felt the same
After you left, I tried to enjoy
The peace and quiet with a
Warm coffee in hand, but it
All seemed pointless alone.

Same with sunsets, it felt
Uncomfortable sitting there
Waiting for the skies to change
And for the sun to set, still
I tried it alone, watching.

But nighttime, that was the
Same for me, soaking in the
Moonlight, feeling the stars
Watch over me, that feeling
That there's something more.

Under an expansive blanket
Of stars I feel hopeful, either
With you or alone, and in the
Silence, I smile as my heart
Heals in the beautiful darkness.

Brianna Malotke

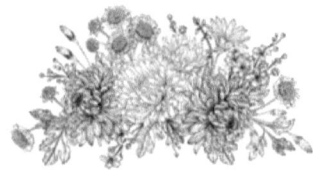

On All the Petals

Wishing, eyes closed tight,
Holding the flowers, discarded
Just like me, I sit by the broken
Fountain, the water more just
A drizzle yet still tranquil.
As I pull—gently—each petal
Off the flowers, I toss them
Into the fountain, wishing
With each one that I'd find
Just a little touch of happiness
In my future. That perhaps
With the next love, I'd find
The one to love with my
Whole soul and they too
Would feel the same, and as

I toss the petals—gently—I
Watch them float, mingling
In the water with the others.
Everything seems peaceful
And my smile genuine, I'm
Feeling hopeful once more.

Brianna Malotke

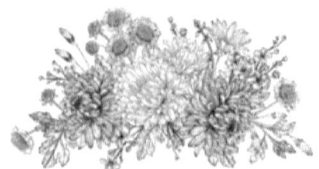

Our Fixed Future

The porcelain teacup fell from
my hands, shattering on impact
as it hit the tile floor.

You had just walked through
the door. My heart raced, as I
stared into your silver eyes.

I thought I'd never see you again,
despite your promises to find
a way to make it back to me.

You took my hand, pulling me
to my feet, and embraced me.

Don't Cry on Cashmere

The pure joy I felt feeling your
heartbeat next to mine was second
only to the kiss that followed.

Holding me tight, telling me everything
That I had been dreaming about for months,
I'm stunned and speechless, but thrilled.

I can't believe you're here with me
Now and that our future, once dismal
And stormy, with nothing on the

Horizon, is in full bloom and we
Can smile together, both full of hope.

Brianna Malotke

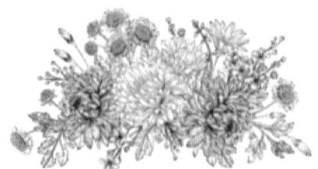

Seasons Changing

Fall used to mean warmth.
Warm, woolen sweaters
Warm, hot cocoa and
Warm, fresh cookies.
Hot apple cider and
Warm fire lit evenings.

Leaves change colors,
The air gets crisp,
And everyone gets ready
For their holiday plans.

But as it is with seasons
Things change.
Autumn turns to winter.
The leaves, ever so bright,
Turn brown and fall.
The air is full of exhaust
And temperatures drop.

She had come to accept
That no one is someone's
Only one forever.
She knew now that
People come and
They may go,
Just like the seasons.

She didn't want to accept
That people could leave
So easily as he did,
Just as the seasons,
But she had to have hope
That someone, someday
Would stay.

Brianna Malotke

Tears from the Night Before

Perfume from yesterday
Clinging to the tearstained pillows
The light from her cigarette
Illuminated the room

Not quite ready to
Welcome the day
She lies in the cold bed
Taking long drags

She knew after one,
Or maybe just two,
Her mind would calm
And her muscles relax

After a shower
And opening the windows
She felt more at peace
Ready to face the day

Broken hearts take time
But with a gorgeous balcony
View of the bustling city
She knew that she'd be fine

Simple as that, she had
All of the time in the world.

Brianna Malotke

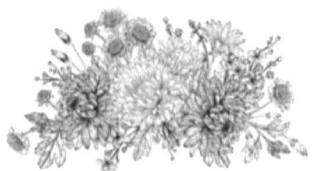

Ready

Pieces broken and scattered
Worried she'll never be whole.

Heart full of longing
Yearning for those never there

She waited night after night
Until she was finally able
To put the pieces back together

With time and acceptance
She was able to be whole

There is darkness in life.
Despite it all
She stands tall
Dreaming of what will come.

With a scarred, full heart
She was ready to love again.

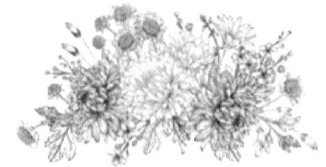

Space for One

Words scrawled across

Dozens of papers

Notes and books

Scattered across her desk

She didn't need the organization

That others so craved

With her physical space

In such disarray

She was able to sit

Soak it all in

Her mind was quiet

Her heart at ease

Brianna Malotke

Don't Cry on Cashmere

Brianna Malotke

BRIANNA MALOTKE is a freelance writer and member of the Horror Writers Association. Ever since she learned to read, she's loved reading and writing. She currently lives with her husband, dog, and two cats in a non-haunted house full of overflowing bookshelves.

While most of her work is within the realms of horror and nightmares, she enjoys writing love poems and drabbles. She has poetry in *The Spectre Review* and *The Nottingham Horror Collective*. You can find more of her horror work in the anthologies *Beautiful Tragedies 2, The Dire Circle*, *Under Her Skin*, *Their Ghoulish Reputation*, and *Out of Time*. As far as love and romance goes, she has numerous pieces in the anthologies *Worlds Apart*, *Out of Time*, and *At First Glance* by Dark Rose Press. Along with these, you can find more of her poetry in the anthologies *Balm*, *Tempest*, and *Cherish* by Ravens Quoth Press. She'll be a "Writer in Residence" at the Chateau d'Orquevaux in France and her first horror poetry collection will be released in 2023.

Find her at: malotkewrites.com

Brianna Malotke

THE RAVENS QUOTH PRESS is a boutique publisher based in Australia, dedicated to showcasing the best of international poetry craft in beautifully presented publications.

Follow us: **linktr.ee/TheRavensQuothPress**

Brianna Malotke

www.ingramcontent.com/pod-product-compliance
Lightning Source LLC
Chambersburg PA
CBHW030302010526
44107CB00053B/1780